DATE DUE

A+
TM
books

Shapes around Town

Ovals
around Town

by Nathan Olson

Capstone
press

Mankato, Minnesota

A+ Books are published by Capstone Press,
151 Good Counsel Drive, P.O. Box 669, Mankato, Minnesota 56002.
www.capstonepress.com

1 2 3 4 5 6 11 10 09 08 07 06

Library of Congress Cataloging-in-Publication Data
Olson, Nathan.
    Ovals around town / by Nathan Olson.
    p. cm.—(A+ books. Shapes around town)
    Summary: "Simple text, photographs, and illustrations help readers identify ovals that can be found in
a city"—Provided by publisher.
    Includes bibliographical references and index.
    ISBN-13: 978-0-7368-6369-8 (hardcover)
    ISBN-10: 0-7368-6369-9 (hardcover)
    1. Ovals—Juvenile literature. 2. Ellipse—Juvenile literature. 3. Geometry, Plane—Juvenile literature. I. Title.
II. Series.
QA485.O47 2007
516'.152—dc22   2006000220

Credits

Jenny Marks, editor; Kia Adams, designer; Renée Doyle, illustrator; Kelly Garvin,
    photo researcher/photo editor

Photo Credits

Capstone Press/Karon Dubke, 21 (boy)
Corbis/Bruce Conolly, 16–17; Carl & Ann Purcell, 10 (sign); Dennis Degnan, 7; Jose Fuste Raga, 18;
    Layne Kennedy, 21 (all but boy); Paul Souders, 9; Philip Gould, 6; Ric Ergenbright, 12; Royalty-Free,
    20; Rudy Sulgan, 8; Tom Stewart, 23; zefa/K. Hackenberg, cover
Getty Images, Inc./Iconica/Brad Wilson, 22; Iconica/Bryan Mullenix, 19; The Image Bank/
    Angelo Cavalli, 11; Stone/Donovan Reese, 14–15
Image Bank, 26–27 (all)
Masterfile/Lloyd Sutton, 4–5
Shutterstock/Dianne Maire, 13; Ingvald Kaldhussater, 10 (door)
SportsChrome, Inc/Rob Tringali, 24–25

Note to Parents, Teachers, and Librarians

The Shapes around Town set uses color photographs and a nonfiction format to introduce readers to
the shapes around them. *Ovals around Town* is designed to be read aloud to a pre-reader, or to be
read independently by an early reader. Images and activities help early readers and listeners perceive
and recognize shapes. The book encourages further learning by including the following sections: Table
of Contents, Which Have Ovals?, Welcome to Oval Town, Glossary, Read More, Internet Sites, and
Index. Early readers may need assistance using these features.

Table of Contents

What Is an Oval?

Ovals are egglike shapes with no corners. Let's look for ovals all around town.

Some ovals look like short, wide circles. Other ovals look like tall, thin circles.

Circles are different from ovals.
A circle is perfectly round.

This oval is tall and thin. It is inside of another shape. Do you know what it is?

You'll see lots of sights through this oval. Trains take people in and out of the city.

These ovals are easy to see. The frames and lenses are both ovals.

The city market sells fruit of all kinds. Do you see any tasty fruits shaped like short, wide ovals?

This oval gives a view
of red and yellow tulips
in the city park.

The postal carrier drops letters through this oval mail slot.

Ovals twist and turn in this curvy red sculpture. Can you find any other shapes here?

Reflecting Ovals

Some ovals are made by reflections.
The water under the bridge acts like
a mirror to make an oval.

Together, an arch and a river
form a reflecting oval.

PULL

Glass doors reflect to make twin ovals of these door handles.

Fun Ovals

Oval mirrors decorate the carnival carousel. Carousel animals that move up and down are called "jumpers."

Oval corn dogs are oh-so delicious. The letter O also has an oval shape.

The playground has lots of fun oval shapes. Even upside down, they still look like ovals.

Lots of little ovals linked together
make a swing's chain.

A zero is an oval shape.
How many zeroes do you
count at this baseball game?

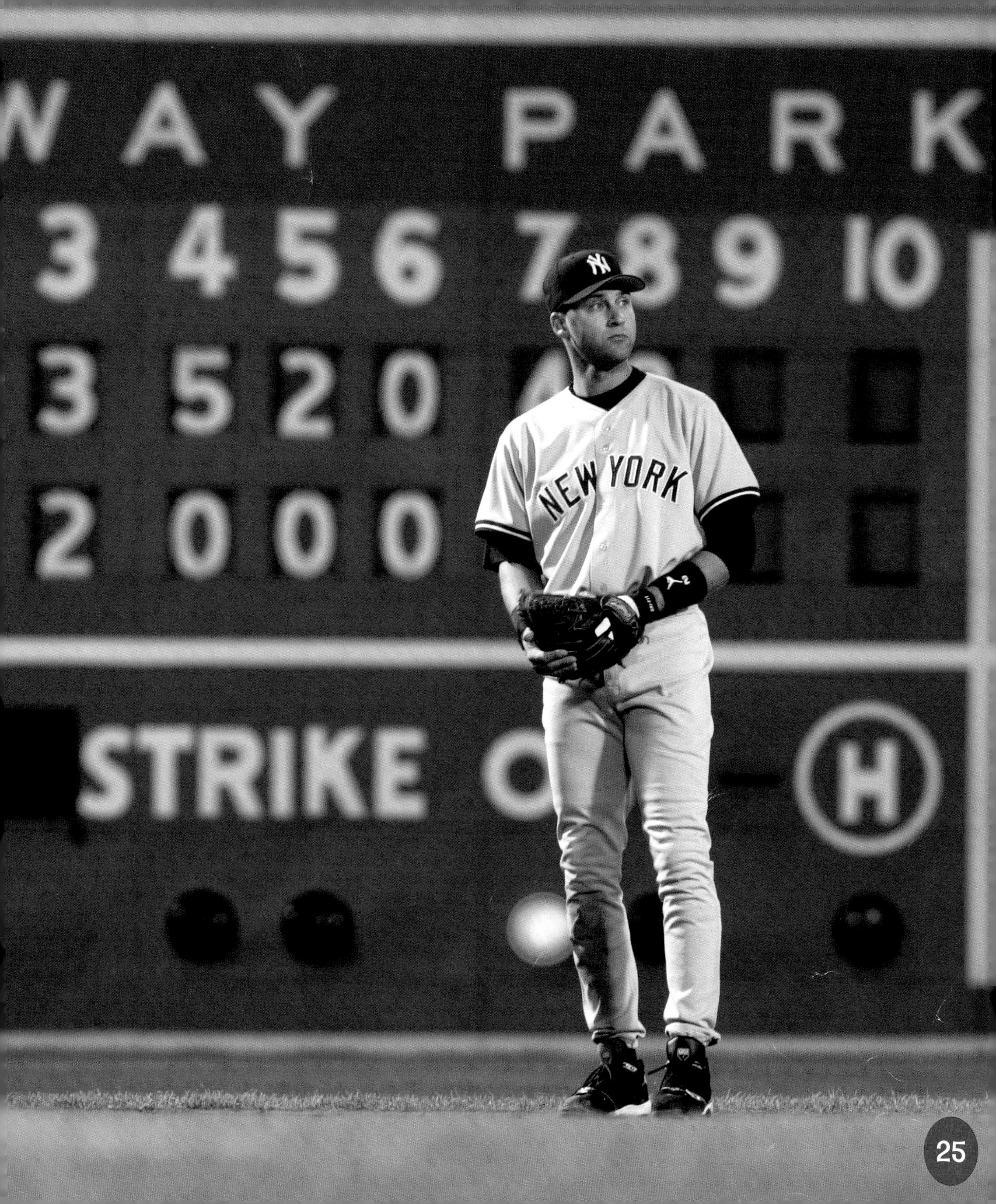
WAY PARK
3 4 5 6 7 8 9 10
3 5 2 0
2 0 0 0
NEW YORK
STRIKE
H

Which Have Ovals?

Ovals are egglike shapes with no corners. Which of these signs have ovals?

ARBORETUM
FIRE STATION
BUSINESS AREA
ELK ST.
JEFFERSON ST
ELIZABETH ST.
40 M.P.H.
ONE WAY

Welcome to Oval Town

Oval Town is full of oval shapes both big and small. Where do you see ovals?

Glossary

arch (ARCH)—a tall, curved structure used for decoration

carnival (KAR-nuh-vuhl)—a public celebration, often with rides, games, and parades

carousel (KAIR-uh-sel)—a ride with wooden or plastic animals on a spinning platform

lens (LENZ)—a piece of curved glass or plastic in a pair of eyeglasses

link (LINGK)—one of the connected ovals that makes up a chain

postal carrier (POHST-uhl KA-ree-uhr)—a person who delivers mail for the post office

sculpture (SKUHLP-chur)—a piece of art carved or shaped out of stone, wood, clay, plastic, or metal

Read More

Burke, Jennifer S. *Ovals*. City Shapes. New York: Children's Press, 2000.

Micklethwait, Lucy. *I Spy Shapes in Art*. New York: Greenwillow Books, 2004.

Schuette, Sarah L. *Ovals*. Shapes. Mankato, Minn.: Capstone Press, 2003.

Internet Sites

FactHound offers a safe, fun way to find Internet sites related to this book. All of the sites on FactHound have been researched by our staff.

Here's how:

1. Go to *www.facthound.com*
2. Select your grade level.
3. Type in this book ID **0736863699** for age-appropriate sites. You may also browse subjects by clicking on the letters, or by clicking on pictures and words.
4. Click on the Fetch It button.

FactHound will fetch the best sites for you!

Index